the spanish cuisine I love

by JULES J. BOND

LEON AMIEL • PUBLISHER
NEW YORK

Published by
LEON AMIEL • PUBLISHER
NEW YORK
ISBN 0-8148-0680-5
©Copyright 1977, by Leon Amiel • Publisher
Printed in the United States of America

Table of Contents

LIST OF COLOR PLATES

Our grateful acknowledgements go to the Spanish Green Olive Commission (SGOC) and Gonzales Byass Sherry (GBS) for providing pictures reproduced in this book. We also extend thanks to the management of Tio Pepe Spanish-Mexican Restaurant (TP), 168 W. 4th Street, N.Y.C., N.Y. They prepared food for us and allowed us to photograph it in their restaurant. Finally we must thank our photographer, Josh Konecky (JK) and Roy Jensen, who coordinated the production of this book.

Foreword

Centuries ago the Spanish brought to the Americas their way of cooking. To a large degree, Mexico and other Latin American countries to this day serve many of the splendid and familiar dishes of Spain.

Immeasurably larger, however, was and still is the influence and importance of Mexican foods in the daily life of the Spanish and indeed most of the world.

Just to mention a few — tomatoes and corn, peppers, squashes, vanilla, avocados and cashews and many others. These are items of everyday foods that were taken back from Mexico to Europe by the Spaniards, along with the potato, although potatoes are not strictly of Mexican origin.

We have tried to include a bit of both in this book; some of the great dishes of Spain and a variety of typical everyday Mexican dishes. We hope you will enjoy them.

Bon appetit

Jules Bond

Notes:

Many markets across America carry Spanish and Mexican foods, packaged, canned or bottled. In some parts of the country, especially the West and the Southwest, most items used in Mexican cooking are readily available. A short guide to some of the foods, especially the confusing variety of chilies (peppers) might be useful.

Chili Powder is a blend of various ground, dried chilies, oregano, cumin and other spices and herbs. It can range from very mild to rather hot, depending on the brand or the blend, and it is advisable to taste it before using the quantities indicated in the following recipes. You may wish to increase or decrease the quantity to be used.

Peppers (chilies) are one of the most important ingredients in Mexican cooking. There are dozens, maybe a hundred varieties, from very mild to fiery hot, and for most people this very abundance can be quite confusing. In many of the recipes in this book chili powder has been substituted for the various peppers one would use in Mexico.

As to the color of peppers, all of them are green or yellowish when unripe and turn into all shades of red or brown when ripened. Their size ranges from the tiniest peppers to some nearly a foot long, and their shapes from round to oval to slim and pointed. Oddly enough, the smallest of the chilies are usually the hottest ones.

Buying canned chilies: *Serrano* and *Jalapeno* chilies are frequently found in stores. Both are quite hot. *Poblano* chilies are mild and are the ones most frequently used in Mexican cooking. Canned California chilies or even green bell peppers are a fair substitute.

Saffron — The only real saffron is the Spanish saffron — dried small threadlike pieces. They are the dried pistils of a member of the crocus family. Saffron is quite expensive but for most dishes the tiniest amount is sufficient. It is best to crumble the amount to be used between a sheet of paper towel, and to dissolve it in a small amount of hot water before adding to the food.

Almond Sauce

2 tbsp. oil
2 tbsp. onion, minced
1 clove garlic, crushed
¼ cup tomato sauce
1 tsp. vinegar

¾ cup chicken broth
1 tsp. parsley, minced
1 tsp. sugar
½ cup blanched almonds, chopped
½ cup dry French bread, cubed

Sauté onion and garlic in oil until light golden, add bread cubes and almonds and sauté another minute. Remove from heat, put in a blender with half of the broth and blend to a paste consistency. Put in a saucepan, add all other ingredients, blend well and simmer for a few minutes. Serve with meat, chicken or fish.

Alli-o-li
(Garlic Mayonnaise)
(1 cup)

4 cloves garlic, crushed
1 tsp. lemon juice
1 tsp. salt
¼ tsp. white pepper

2 tbsp. soft white breadcrumbs
2 egg yolks
1 cup olive oil
1 tbsp. dry sherry (opt.)

Put lemon juice, salt, pepper, garlic, breadcrumbs, and egg yolks in a blender, blend for a few seconds at low speed. Add the oil, drop by drop at first, until the mixture starts to thicken, and then in a thin stream. When mayonnaise has thickened, blend in a spoonful of hot water and the sherry. Serve with broiled seafood or broiled or roast meats.

Chili Sauce

(about 3 cups)

1 medium onion, chopped
2 cloves garlic, minced
4 tbsp. olive oil
3 cups chicken broth
1/3 cup tomato puree
1 tbsp. wine vinegar

1 pinch cayenne pepper
salt to taste
1/2 tsp. oregano
4 to 6 tbsp. chili powder
  (or to taste)
1 1/2 tbsp. cornstarch

Sauté onion and garlic in oil until they just start to take on color. Add chicken broth, tomato puree, vinegar, pepper, salt and oregano, stir well, mix chili powder with a little water and add to sauce. Blend again and simmer for about 45 minutes. Strain sauce through a sieve and return to pan. Correct seasoning. Dissolve cornstarch in a little water, add to sauce and simmer, stirring once in a while until sauce has thickened. Serve with tamales, meat or poultry.

Chili and Tomato Sauce

½ cup onion, minced
2 tbsp. olive oil
3 cups tomato puree
3 cloves garlic, crushed
salt to taste

3 tbsp. chili powder
½ tsp. basil
½ tsp. oregano
¼ tsp. cumin seed, ground

Sauté onion in oil until light golden, add all other ingredients and blend well. Cover and simmer for one hour. Strain and press through a sieve. Serve with enchiladas.

Garlic Sauce
(about 1 cup)

3 tbsp. olive oil
3 cloves garlic, peeled
1 tbsp. onion, grated
2 cloves garlic, minced
3 tbsp. parsley
salt and pepper to taste

¼ tsp. dried marjoram
½ tsp. tarragon
½ cup fresh orange juice
2 tbsp. lemon juice
1 tbsp. lime juice

Sauté 3 whole garlic cloves in oil until browned. Remove and discard garlic. Add minced garlic and onion, sauté for a minute, add all other ingredients, bring to a simmer and simmer for 2 or 3 minutes. Serve over sautéed fish or chicken breasts.

Green Sauce

(about 1 cup)

3 large ripe tomatoes, peeled,
  seeded
1 medium onion, chopped
1 clove garlic, minced
½ small green hot chili pepper
  or to taste (canned chili
  can be used)

¼ tsp. oregano
¼ tsp. ground coriander
1 tbsp. lime juice
salt and pepper to taste

   Place all ingredients in a blender or food processor and blend until smooth. Use with meats, tacos or enchiladas.

Parsley Sauce
(about ½ cup)

¾ cup minced parsley
¼ cup blanched almonds, chopped
1 clove garlic, minced

6 tbsp. olive oil
4 tbsp. white wine vinegar
salt and pepper to taste
pinch of cayenne pepper (opt.)

Put all ingredients in a blender or food processor and blend until smooth. Serve with fish, chicken or meat, or as a dip with raw vegetables.

Taco Sauce

3 cups canned tomatoes,
   measured, drained, chopped
6 scallions, chopped
1 clove garlic, minced
¼ tsp. coriander, ground

½ tsp. oregano
1 tbsp. olive oil
1 tbsp. vinegar
2 green chili peppers
   (or to taste) chopped
salt to taste

Combine all ingredients and blend well. Simmer for a few minutes. Serve hot or cold.

Tomato Sauce

(about 3 cups)

1 ½ lbs. ripe tomatoes, peeled,
   seeded and chopped
1 medium onion, minced
1 clove garlic, minced
2 tbsp. olive oil
1 cup beef broth
1 ½ tsp. oregano

1 tsp. basil
pinch of thyme
1 small bay leaf
2 tsp. sugar
1 tbsp. lemon juice
salt and pepper to taste

Sauté onions and garlic in oil until soft and starting to take on color. Add all other ingredients and simmer for about 30 minutes.

Nachos

Nachos are small tostadas *(p. 95)* served as appetizers with a great variety of fillings. Fried like tostadas in deep fat, they can be spread with fried beans, grilled cheese and chili peppers, chopped meat and others.

Nachos.→

Marinated Shrimp with Olives and Mushrooms

(for 6)

1 lb. fresh, firm mushrooms,
  quartered
1 cup water
$^1/_3$ cup olive oil
$^2/_3$ cup vinegar
2 tbsp. lemon juice
2 cloves garlic, halved
salt to taste
$^1/_2$ tsp. thyme

$^1/_2$ tsp. black peppercorns
pinch of grated nutmeg
pinch of cayenne pepper
2 bay leaves
¾ cup pimiento-stuffed
  green Spanish olives
2 lbs. medium shrimp, cleaned
  and cooked

Combine mushrooms, water, oil, vinegar, lemon juice and seasonings in a saucepan. Bring to a boil, cover and cook for 5 minutes. Pour into a bowl, add olives and shrimp, toss and cool. Chill for a few hours or overnight before serving.

Note: Do not overcook shrimp. Put them in cold water, bring to a boil and simmer for 1 minute. Let cool in the cooking liquid.

←*Marinated Shrimp with Olives and Mushrooms.*

Bean Dip
(for 4)

1 cup refried beans (p. 114)   1 tsp. dijon mustard
¾ cup sour cream   1 tsp. lemon juice
1 tbsp. grated onion   salt and pepper to taste

Blend all ingredients and let stand for an hour or so before serving.

Spiced Cashew Nuts

1 lb. salted cashew nuts
2 large cloves garlic,
   minced

6 or 7 small red chili
   peppers
1 tbsp. olive oil
1 tsp. chili powder

    Heat oil in a heavy skillet, add garlic and chilies and sauté for a minute, stirring constantly. Add cashews, stir and blend and sauté over medium heat for about 4 minutes. Shake the pan and stir occasionally while sautéing. Sprinkle with chili powder, blend well, cool and put in a glass jar. Let stand for at least a day before serving.

Chorizo Canapés

4 chorizo sausages
  (about ½ lb.)
1 small can tomato paste
2 tbsp. grated onion
½ tsp. basil

1 small clove garlic, minced
1½ tsp. chili powder
grated romano or parmesan
  cheese
thin slices of French bread

    Strip sausages from casings, break up meat with a fork and sauté in a heavy skillet without adding any fat until the meat is browned. Add tomato paste, onion, basil, garlic and chili powder, blend well and simmer for 5 minutes. Spread on bread slices, sprinkle with a goodly amount of cheese and put under a medium broiler until top is bubbly and browned.

Garlic Eggs
(for 6)

1 large clove garlic,
  crushed
3 anchovy filets, mashed
1 tsp. capers, chopped
1 tsp. chili powder

1 tsp. lemon juice
4 tbsp. olive oil
salt and pepper to taste
6 hard-boiled eggs

    Combine all ingredients except eggs and blend well. Quarter the eggs, coat with the garlic sauce.

Avocado Cream

(about 2 cups)

1 avocado, peeled and pit
  removed
²/₃ cup sour cream
½ cup mayonnaise
2 tbsp. parsley, minced
1 tbsp. paprika

1 tbsp. onion, grated
1 small clove garlic,
  crushed
1 tbsp. lime juice
1 pinch cayenne pepper
salt and pepper to taste

Put all ingredients in a blender or food processor and blend until very smooth. Use as a dip or on fish, cold meats or salads.

Guacamole

(for 4)

2 ripe avocados
2 medium tomatoes, peeled,
   seeded and chopped
2 tbsp. grated onion
2 green chili peppers
   (fresh or canned) chopped

1 tbsp. olive oil
1 tbsp. lemon juice
1 tbsp. lime juice
salt and pepper to taste
½ tsp. ground coriander
   (opt.)

    Mash peeled avocados with a fork, blend in lemon and lime juice, and then all other ingredients.

Cocktail Meat Balls

2 tbsp. minced onion
1 small clove garlic,
  minced
1 tbsp. butter
2 tsp. chili powder
¼ tsp. ground coriander
¾ lb. lean beef, ground
¼ lb. lean pork, ground
oil for frying

¾ cup fine dry breadcrumbs
  (sifted if too coarse)
1 egg, beaten
¼ cup light cream
¼ cup water
1 tbsp. parsley, chopped
salt and pepper to taste
pinch of tabasco pepper

Sauté onion and garlic in butter until soft but not browned, stir in chili powder and coriander, and remove from fire. Combine with all other ingredients and form mixture into very small balls, the size of a marble. Fry in oil until well browned, drain on paper towel and keep warm until serving.

Stuffed Cocktail Meat Balls

1 lb. ground lean beef
1 egg, beaten
½ tsp. chili powder

salt and pepper to taste
pimiento-stuffed green olives
oil for frying

Blend beef, egg, chili powder, salt and pepper. Shape meat around each olive to make a ball double the size of the olive. Fry in oil until well browned on all sides or brush with oil and broil in oven or over charcoal.

Small firm button mushrooms can be used instead of olives. Marinate mushrooms for half an hour in oil and lemon juice before using.

Seviche

1 lb. mild fish filets
   (haddock, weakfish, whiting,
   or scallops instead of fish)
½ cup fresh lemon juice
½ cup fresh lime juice
1 cup peeled and diced
   ripe tomatoes
4 small hot chilies (red or
   green), diced

1 medium onion, minced
¼ cup olive oil
¼ cup dry white wine
½ tsp. oregano
¼ tsp. ground coriander
½ tsp. sweet basil
1 tbsp. parsley, minced
salt and pepper to taste

Cut fish in squares or dice scallops, put in a bowl, cover with lemon and lime juice and let stand for about 3 hours. Turn once in a while. Then add all other ingredients, mix and chill well for several hours before serving. Garnish with thinly sliced Bermuda onion and parsley sprigs.

Shrimp Cocktail
(for 4)

1 lb. medium shrimp
¼ cup dry white wine
3 tbsp. lime juice
¼ tsp. grated lime rind

1 tsp. grated onion
⅓ cup ketchup
salt to taste
tabasco sauce to taste

Put shrimp in cold salted water, bring to boil, simmer for 2 minutes. Cool slightly, shell and devein. Blend all other ingredients, pour over shrimp, blend and refrigerate for several hours before serving.

Marinated Shrimp

(for 6)

1 ½ lbs. medium shrimps,
  cooked and deveined
1 medium ripe tomato, peeled,
  seeded and minced
2 tbsp. dijon mustard
2 tsp. prepared horseradish

2 tbsp. lime juice
¾ cup olive oil
1 tsp. chili powder
pinch of cayenne pepper
salt and pepper to taste
¾ cup white wine vinegar

Combine all ingredients, pour over shrimp, blend well and marinate for several hours before serving.

Shrimp Ajillo

(for 12 appetizer servings)

10 garlic cloves, peeled
¼ cup olive oil
2 lbs. medium shrimp, peeled
  and deveined
2 bay leaves

¼ cup dry sherry
½ tsp. salt
½ tsp. celery salt
pinch of cayenne pepper
alli-o-li *(p. 8)*

In a large skillet brown garlic cloves in oil. Add shrimp and bay leaves. Sauté over high heat until shrimp are cooked — about 3 to 4 minutes — stirring and shaking the pan. Stir in sherry, salt, celery salt and cayenne pepper. Remove from heat, stir in Alli-o-li by the large spoonfuls and serve immediately.

Devilled Shrimp
(for 6)

1½ lbs. shrimp, cooked,
   shelled and deveined
4 tbsp. sherry
½ cup dry white wine
⅓ cup white wine vinegar
1½ tsp. prepared horseradish
1½ tbsp. dijon mustard

1 tbsp. paprika
tabasco sauce to taste
¼ tsp. ground cardamon
2 tbsp. tomato paste
1½ tsp. sugar
1 clove garlic, crushed
salt to taste

Combine all ingredients except shrimp, blend well. Pour over shrimp, mix, cover and marinate for a few hours. For serving, drain shrimp and serve marinade on the side if desired.

Shrimp Rolls

¾ lb. shrimp
1 egg, lightly beaten
1 cup white breadcrumbs
salt and pepper to taste
1 small clove garlic,
   crushed

2 tbsp. olive oil
¼ cup dry white wine
¼ cup tomato juice
1 tsp. dill weed
1 tsp. chili powder
1 tsp. dijon mustard

   Put shrimp in cold water, bring to a boil and remove immediately. Drain, shell and devein shrimp. Cool slightly and chop them very fine. Blend well with all other ingredients, chill for 2 or 3 hours. Then shape into small rolls the size of a finger, broil under medium flame for about 5 or 6 minutes, turning once.

Gazpacho Andaluz
(for 6)

4 cups day-old French or
   Italian bread or hard
   rolls, cubed
chicken broth
1½ cups pared and diced
   cucumber
1 medium green pepper,
   seeded and diced

2 cloves garlic
2 tsp. salt
½ cup olive oil
¼ cup wine vinegar
2 lbs. fresh ripe tomatoes,
   seeded and cubed
ice cubes

Accompaniments:

sliced stuffed Spanish olives
diced cucumber
chopped scallions
diced green pepper

crumbled crisp bacon
toasted slivered almonds
diced tomatoes
chopped hard-boiled eggs

   Place bread cubes in a shallow dish and add broth 1 inch deep. Let bread soak, turning once.
   Combine cucumber, green pepper, garlic, salt, oil and vinegar in an electric blender or in a food processor, blend smooth. Add half of the bread cubes and blend smooth again. Pour mixture into a bowl. Mix remaining bread and tomatoes and add to the bowl. Correct seasoning adding more salt and vinegar if desired. Chill well. When serving place one or two ice cubes in each soup bowl, serve with accompaniments.

Gazpacho Andaluz.→

Garlic Soup I

(for 4)

4 tbsp. olive oil
5 large cloves garlic,
  peeled
4 slices of French bread,
  crust trimmed off

1 tbsp. parsley, minced
¼ tsp. hot red pepper
salt to taste
4 poached eggs
4 cups hot beef broth

Put oil in a saucepan, add garlic and sauté gently until garlic is golden brown. Remove garlic, crush with a fork and reserve. Sauté bread slices in the oil, add beef broth, crushed garlic, parsley, pepper and salt. Stir well, let soup come to a simmer. Put one poached egg into each soup plate, ladle soup over it and serve.

←*Garlic Soup.*

Garlic Soup II

(for 8)

16 cloves of garlic
1 quart boiling water
2 quarts chicken broth
¼ tsp. ground sage
¼ tsp. thyme
1 small bay leaf
4 sprigs parsley
2 whole cloves
3 tbsp. olive oil

3 cups diced raw potatoes
¼ tsp. Spanish saffron
salt and pepper to taste
¾ cup pimiento-stuffed
   Spanish olives, sliced
rounds of toasted French
   bread
1 cup grated gruyere or
   parmesan cheese

Drop unpeeled cloves of garlic into boiling water. Boil for a minute, drain and cool garlic under running water. Peel the cloves. In a large saucepan combine garlic, chicken broth, herbs, cloves and olive oil. Bring to a boil, cover and simmer for 30 minutes. Strain and return strained soup to saucepan; add saffron, potatoes, salt and pepper. Bring to a boil and simmer, covered, for 20 minutes or until potatoes are just soft. Add olives and heat through. Add toasted French bread to each bowl and sprinkle with grated cheese.

Avocado Soup

(for 6)

1 medium tomato, peeled,
    seeded and chopped
1 tbsp. minced onion
4 cups chicken broth
½ cup heavy cream

¼ cup dry sherry
salt and pepper to taste
1 tsp. lemon juice
2 large avocados

    Put all ingredients except avocados and sherry in a blender, or blend well with a whisk, heat in a saucepan and simmer for a few minutes. Peel and mash avocados, blend into the soup, add sherry, heat through and serve. This soup can also be served cold.

Cold Avocado and Tomato Soup
(for 6)

1 cup cucumber, peeled
  diced
¼ cup red onion, minced
½ cup sweet pepper, minced
1 small avocado, diced
2 cups tomato juice
1 cup chicken broth

2 tbsp. olive oil
1 tbsp. lime juice
2 tbsp. wine vinegar
½ tbsp. oregano
pinch of cayenne pepper
salt and pepper to taste

Put all ingredients in a serving bowl, blend and chill well. Serve in individual soup bowls, top each bowl with a thin slice of onion and put an ice cube in each bowl.

Bean Soup

(for 4)

1 cup kidney or pinto beans
4 cups chicken broth
1 medium onion, sliced
1 green pepper, minced
1 large tomato, peeled,
    seeded and chopped

salt and pepper to taste
1 tsp. chili powder
¼ tsp. powdered coriander
1 tsp. oregano
fried bread croutons

Soak beans overnight in cold water. Drain, bring chicken broth to a boil, add beans and cook for at least 4 hours, the longer the better. After 2 hours cooking add all other ingredients. When beans are soft, rub soup through a sieve or puree in a blender. Reheat and add more broth if necessary. Serve with fried croutons.

Chick Pea Soup

(for 6)

½ lb. dried chick peas
1 smoked pigs knuckle
1 beef or veal bone
4 cups beef broth
4 cups water
¼ lb. salt pork, diced
salt and pepper to taste

1 medium onion, minced
1 clove garlic, minced
1 tbsp. paprika
6 medium potatoes, peeled
  and quartered
½ lb. garlic sausage,
  sliced

Soak chick peas overnight in cold water to cover. Drain, add broth and water, pigs knuckle, beef bone, salt and pepper. Cover and simmer for an hour or more until peas are nearly cooked. Fry salt pork, then add onion, garlic and paprika, stir and sauté for 3 or 4 minutes, then add to the chick peas and simmer for one half hour longer. Remove bones and pigs knuckle; take meat off pigs knuckle, dice and return to pot along with potatoes. Cook until potatoes are done, add sausage and heat through.

Cocido

(for 6)

A Cocido is really a full meal and nothing else needs to be served. It is one of the classic dishes of Spain and all the Latin countries in America.

1 cup chick peas
8 cups chicken or beef broth
1 lb. beef shoulder
 (cut into large cubes)
1 lb. boneless lamb, cubed
1 small broiling chicken,
 cut up
1 beef marrow bone
1 onion, sliced
salt and pepper to taste

1 tomato, peeled, seeded,
 chopped
2 carrots, peeled and sliced
1 stalk celery, sliced
2 white turnips, diced
3 zucchini, sliced
3 cloves garlic, peeled
 and cut in half
2 chorizo sausages (opt.)

Soak chick peas overnight in cold water. Drain and rub off the skins. Bring broth to a boil, add chick peas, beef, lamb, marrow bone, and simmer for about 1 hour. Add chicken and chorizos and continue cooking for another 15 minutes. Then add all vegetables, salt and pepper and cook for another 15 minutes or until vegetables are tender.

Clam Soup
(for 4)

2 dozen clams
1 cup minced onion
2 cloves garlic, minced
4 tbsp. olive oil
clam juice and water to
   make 4 cups liquid

4 tbsp. sherry
4 tbsp. parsley, minced
⅛ tsp. Spanish saffron
2 tbsp. tomato paste
salt and pepper to taste

Scrub clams, put 1 cup boiling water in a saucepan, add clams, cover and cook until the shells open. Remove the clams from shells and chop. Strain clam juice.

Sauté onion and garlic in oil until soft but not browned. Add sherry, parsley and tomato paste, mix and add all other ingredients, blend well, bring to a simmer and simmer for 5 minutes before serving.

Corn Soup

(for 4)

3 cups fresh sweet corn
  kernels
½ cup light cream
½ cup scallions, chopped
1 small clove garlic, chopped
4 cups chicken broth

1 small green pepper,
  diced small
4 tbsp. parsley, chopped
2 tbsp. flour
2 tbsp. butter
salt and pepper to taste

Put corn, cream, garlic and scallions and 1 cup broth in a blender or food processor and blend until smooth. Heat remaining broth in a saucepan, add the pureed corn mixture, green pepper, parsley, salt and pepper. Bring to a boil and simmer for 15 minutes. Melt butter in a saucepan, stir in flour and cook, stirring for a few minutes. Do not let roux brown. Then stir in some of the soup, blend well and add to the rest of the soup. Blend well and simmer until the soup thickens.

Gazpacho
(for 4 to 6)

1 cucumber, peeled and diced

1 red onion, minced

1 clove garlic, minced

2 large tomatoes, peeled,
seeded and cut into chunks

1 green pepper, seeded and
diced

2 cups tomato juice

1 cup chicken broth

¼ cup wine vinegar

1 tsp. oregano

salt and pepper to taste

pinch of cayenne pepper

Combine all ingredients, chill well for a few hours. When serving, put a cube of ice into each soup bowl.

Tortilla Soup
(for 4)

½ cup lean bacon, chopped
1 medium onion, chopped
1 clove garlic, minced
1 small green pepper,
   seeded and diced
1 small chili pepper, minced

4 tortillas, cut in strips
½ tsp. oregano
4 cups chicken broth
salt and pepper to taste
¼ cup grated parmesan cheese
¼ cup grated cheddar cheese

    Sauté bacon in a saucepan for a few minutes until lightly browned. Add onions, garlic and green pepper, sauté for 5 minutes, stirring occasionally. Add chili and tortilla strips and sauté 3 minutes longer. Add broth and seasonings, bring to a boil and simmer for a few minutes. Ladle soup into individual, ovenproof bowls, sprinkle combined cheeses on top and bake in a 475⁰ oven for about 5 minutes or until cheese topping is browned.

Baked Eggs Ibiza

(for 4)

8 eggs
2 tbsp. butter
1½ cups tomato, peeled,
  seeded and chopped
2 tbsp. parsley, minced
1 tbsp. chives, minced

salt and pepper to taste
4 Italian sausages (sweet
  or hot according to
  taste)
2 tbsp. grated parmesan cheese
paprika

Simmer sausages for a few minutes in water, then fry them until browned. Butter a shallow baking dish, cover the bottom with tomatoes, sprinkle with parsley and chives, season with salt and pepper. Break eggs carefully on top of tomatoes, slice sausages lengthwise in half and arrange around eggs. Sprinkle with cheese and paprika and bake in 375⁰ oven for about 5 minutes until eggs are well set.

Eggs and Sausage
(for 4)

2 or 3 chorizos *(p. 93)*
1 green pepper, seeded
  and diced
1 small onion, minced

1 tbsp. oil
4 eggs
salt to taste

    Remove sausages from casing, break up sausages, sauté in oil for 3 or 4 minutes, stirring occasionally. Then add pepper and onion and sauté another 2 or 3 minutes, until vegetables are soft. Add lightly beaten eggs, salt, blend with the other ingredients in pan and scramble until done to taste.

Mexican Omelet
(for 2)

4 eggs, lightly beaten
1 small onion, minced
1 tbsp.green olives,
  chopped

1 tbsp. canned pimiento,
  chopped
1½ tbsp. butter
salt and pepper to taste

Blend lightly beaten eggs with onion, olives and pimiento, salt and pepper. Heat butter in an omelet pan, pour in the egg mixture, and proceed as if cooking a regular omelet.

Ranchero Eggs

(for 4)

3 tbsp. oil
4 tortillas
1 tbsp. onion, minced
1 small clove garlic,
   minced
½ tsp. basil
½ tsp. marjoram

1 tbsp. parsley, minced
½ tsp. ground coriander
salt and pepper to taste
1 cup tomato sauce
8 eggs (poached or fried)
1 small avocado, sliced
canned pimiento

Fry tortillas in oil, set aside and keep hot. Add onion and garlic to the same oil, sauté for a minute or so, add all other ingredients except eggs, avocado and pimiento. Blend and simmer for 2 or 3 minutes. Then place 2 eggs on each tortilla, cover the eggs with sauce and top with slices of avocado and pieces of pimiento.

Acapulco Omelet

(for 2 to 3)

1 large avocado
8 eggs

salt and pepper to taste
1 tbsp. oil
2 tbsp. butter

Peel the avocado, cut in half, and remove the pit. Dice one half and cut the other half with a melon baller into small balls.

Beat the eggs with salt and pepper to taste, add the diced avocado. Heat oil and butter in a skillet, add the eggs and make a flat omelet, turning it over with a large spatula when the eggs begin to set, and finish cooking.

Place the omelet on a hot serving dish and garnish with the avocado balls.

Acapulco Omelet.→

Sauced Eggs
(for 4)

2 tbsp. onions, minced

2 tbsp. butter

¼ cup milk

1 tbsp. cornstarch

2 avocados

pinch of cayenne pepper

salt and pepper to taste

8 hard-boiled eggs

chopped parsley

Sauté onions in butter until transparent. Dissolve cornstarch in milk and add to onions, stir to thicken. Mash avocados through a sieve and add to onions and milk. Blend well and simmer for a few minutes until mixture is hot and smooth. Season with cayenne, salt and pepper.

While preparing the above, boil the eggs, remove shell and keep hot. When the sauce is ready, cut the eggs in quarters, put them on a serving dish and coat with the avocado sauce. Sprinkle with chopped parsley.

←*Tortilla Soup* — See page 47 for recipe.

Scrambled Eggs

(for 2)

4 eggs

2 tbsp. heavy cream

1 tbsp. butter

1 sweet green pepper,
   seeded and minced

1 small ripe tomato, peeled,
   seeded and chopped

2 scallions, minced

2 tsp. chili powder

pinch of cayenne pepper

¼ tsp. lemon juice

salt to taste

1 tbsp. parsley, minced

Beat eggs and cream lightly and set aside. Sauté green pepper in butter until soft, add all other ingredients except eggs and parsley and simmer for 2 or 3 minutes. Then add eggs and scramble over gentle heat while stirring. Add parsley just before serving. The eggs should be quite creamy.

Tortilla and Eggs
(for 2)

1 tortilla
2 tbsp. oil
1 tbsp. butter
2 eggs, beaten
2 tbsp. milk
salt and pepper to taste

½ tsp. paprika
¼ tsp. chili powder
½ small clove garlic, crushed
2 tbsp. parmesan cheese,
  grated

Heat oil and butter in a skillet. Cut tortilla into wedges and sauté until soft. Blend all other ingredients, pour over tortilla and cook as you would a plain open omelet.

Bacalao
(Salt Codfish)
(for 4)

1 lb. salt cod
flour
$^1/_3$ cup olive oil
1 large onion, minced
2 cloves garlic, minced
1 bay leaf
salt and pepper to taste

3 ripe tomatoes, peeled,
   seeded and chopped
½ tsp. basil
3 tbsp. pimiento, chopped
a few threads of saffron
2 tbsp. parsley, chopped

Soak codfish for 8 hours in cold water. Change water 2 or 3 times. Drain fish, dry with paper towels, cut fish in strips, dust with flour and sauté in oil until golden brown. Remove from pan and reserve. Add onion to pan and sauté until soft, do not let brown. Return fish to pan, add all other ingredients, blend and simmer on top of stove for about 45 minutes or until fish is cooked; or cover and cook in a preheated 350⁰ oven.

Escabeche
(for 4)

2 lbs. fish filets
¼ cup olive oil
1 tbsp. grated onion
2 scallions, minced
1 bay leaf, crumbled
1 small clove garlic,
   crushed

2 green chilis (canned),
   chopped
2 tbsp. pimiento (chopped)
¼ cup wine vinegar
juice of 1 large orange
1 tbsp. lime juice
salt and pepper to taste

    Sauté fish in olive oil until lightly browned on both sides. Remove fish to a serving dish, add all other ingredients to pan, blend and heat for a minute, then pour over fish. Chill well before serving. Garnish with olives, lettuce leaves, and strips of pimiento.

Fish in Orange Juice

(for 4)

4 fish filets
salt and pepper to taste
¼ cup lime juice
4 tbsp. olive oil
2 scallions, minced
1 small clove garlic, crushed
½ cup orange juice

1 large, very ripe tomato,
   peeled, seeded and
   chopped
2 tbsp. pimiento (canned), diced
2 tbsp. capers, drained
   and chopped
2 tbsp. dry sherry

Put fish in a shallow dish, sprinkle with salt, pepper and lime juice on both sides and let stand for 15 minutes. Grease a shallow baking dish with some of the oil, place fish on top, combine scallions, garlic, tomato, pimiento and capers and spread the mixture on top of fish filets. Sprinkle with remaining oil and bake in 350⁰ oven for 10 minutes. Then pour orange juice and sherry over fish and bake another 10 to 15 minutes or until fish is done.

Gulf Fish Stew
(for 4)

2 lbs. firm fish filets
2 large sweet onions,
  sliced thin
¼ cup parsley, minced
1 sweet green pepper,
  seeded and minced

1 tsp. chili powder
tabasco (or other pepper
  sauce) to taste
salt to taste
1 ½ cups dry white wine
1 cup water

Cover bottom of a casserole with onion rings, place a layer of filets on top. Sprinkle with a mixture of all other ingredients except wine and water. Cover with more filets, onion slices and the rest of the seasoning mixture. Pour the wine over it and add just enough water to have liquid come to the top of the fish. Cover very tightly, bring to a boil and simmer for about 15 minutes.

Zarzuela

(for 6)

1 lb. fresh codfish
1 lb. striped bass
¾ lb. eel, skinned
6 large shrimp, cooked
1 lb. mussels
4 small squid (opt.)
6 tbsp. olive oil
2 tbsp. butter
2 onions, thinly sliced
¾ cup tomato puree

4 cups dry white wine
1 tbsp. rum
salt and pepper to taste
1 clove garlic, minced
½ cup fresh white breadcrumbs
⅛ tsp. Spanish saffron
½ cup minced parsley
12 blanched almonds
12 triangles of white
   bread, fried in hot oil
   until golden

Cut the codfish, bass and eel into thick pieces. Shell the cooked shrimp and set them aside. Scrub the mussels and cook in a tightly covered pot over high heat until the shells open. Remove from shells, discard any that have not opened. Add mussels to shrimp. Strain and reserve all the mussel juice. Wash squid and cut them in pieces.

Heat half the oil and all the butter in a large skillet, sauté the onions until they are soft. Add the eel, squid, tomato puree, wine and rum. Bring to a boil and cook over high heat for about 10 minutes. Pour the contents of the skillet into a large casserole, add half of the mussel liquid, mix well.

Add remaining oil to the skillet and cook the pieces of codfish and bass in it for about 3 minutes or until the flesh begins to firm. Season with salt and pepper and add fish to casserole. Simmer covered for 20 minutes but do not let boil.

Mix garlic, breadcrumbs, saffron and half the parsley. Add the remaining mussel liquid and mix until smooth. Add this mixture and almonds to casserole. Blend carefully so as not to break the fish. Finally add the mussels and shrimp, cook for 2 minutes and correct seasoning. Sprinkle with remaining parsley, decorate with bread triangles and serve directly from the casserole.

Baked Red Snapper
(for 4)

2 lb. red snapper
(or sea bass or other fish),
cleaned and scaled
1 clove garlic, crushed
2 tsp. salt
4 tbsp. olive oil
1 medium onion, minced
3 large tomatoes, peeled,
seeded and chopped

¼ tsp. allspice
¼ tsp. coriander, ground
pinch of cayenne pepper
½ green pepper, chopped
2 tbsp. green olives,
chopped
1 tbsp. capers, drained
and chopped
1 tbsp. lime juice

Wipe fish inside and out with paper towel. Combine garlic and salt and rub fish inside and out with this mixture.

Sauté onion in oil until golden. Add tomatoes, allspice, coriander and cayenne and simmer for 5 minutes. Put fish in an oiled baking dish, sprinkle pepper, olives, capers and lime juice over it. Cover with the tomato and onion mixture and bake in a 350⁰ oven for about 30 minutes or until fish is cooked and flaky.

Shrimp Casserole
(for 4)

1 lb. large shrimp,
   peeled and deveined
3 tbsp. olive oil
2 tomatoes, peeled, seeded
   and diced
1 sweet green pepper,
   seeded and diced

1 small onion, minced
1 clove garlic, minced
½ tsp. basil
¼ tsp. oregano
cayenne pepper to taste
salt and pepper to taste

Sauté onions and garlic in oil until soft but not browned. Add all other vegetables and seasonings, blend and simmer covered for 10 minutes. Cut shrimp lengthwise in half, add to the vegetables, cover and simmer very gently for 10 minutes.

Broiled Savory Chicken
(for 4)

2 broiling chickens, split, breastbone removed
1 tbsp. salt
2 tbsp. paprika
¼ tsp. crushed hot red pepper
3 tbsp. oil
1 clove garlic, crushed
3 tbsp. hot chili peppers (canned) diced
½ cup lime juice
1 onion, sliced paper thin
sprigs of parsley

Have butcher flatten the chicken halves with a cleaver. Wipe chicken with a damp cloth. Combine salt, paprika, hot pepper and oil, and rub into the chicken. Place chicken in a shallow dish. Combine garlic, chili peppers and the lime juice, pour over chicken. Place in refrigerator and marinate overnight. Turn the chicken a couple of times.

Remove from refrigerator a couple of hours before cooking. Broil over charcoal, basting with the marinade and turning it frequently until done. Garnish with onion slices and parsley.

Chicken Casserole
(for 4)

1 frying chicken (3 lbs.) cut
   in serving pieces
¼ cup oil
2 tbsp. butter
flour, seasoned with salt,
   pepper and paprika
5 strips lean bacon, diced
2 carrots, peeled and sliced
1 small onion, sliced

1 can green chili peppers,
   cut in strips
1 small bay leaf
1 tbsp. parsley, minced
¼ tsp. rosemary, crumbled
⅛ tsp. thyme
1 lemon, thinly sliced
1 cup dry white wine
1 cup tomato juice

Dredge chicken pieces in seasoned flour. Heat oil and butter in a skillet and sauté chicken pieces until browned on all sides. Remove chicken and place in a casserole. Add all other ingredients except lemon, wine and tomato juice. Sprinkle with 2 tablespoons of the seasoned flour. Arrange sliced lemon on top of chicken, add wine and tomato juice, cover and bake in 350⁰ oven for about one hour or until chicken is tender. Correct the seasoning of sauce and serve.

Cold Chicken in Marinade
(for 4)

1 frying chicken (3 lbs.)
4 tbsp. olive oil
1½ cups dry white wine
2 tbsp. lemon juice
1 tbsp. vinegar
1 lemon, thinly sliced

2 bay leaves
⅛ tsp. thyme
¼ tsp. grated lemon rind
1 tbsp. capers, chopped
salt and crushed pepper
   to taste

Truss chicken. Heat oil in a skillet and brown chicken on all sides. Place chicken in a deep casserole. Blend all other ingredients, except sliced lemon, pour over chicken and bring to a boiling point on top of the stove. Cover the casserole and cook in a preheated 350^0 oven for one hour or until chicken is tender. Let chicken cool in the marinade and then chill for a day before serving. Garnish with lemon slices.

Chicken in Orange Juice
and Pineapple
(for 4)

1 cup orange juice
½ cup raisins
1 frying chicken (3½ lbs.)
  cut into serving pieces
flour
3 tbsp. oil
⅓ cup blanched almonds,
  slivered

½ cup crushed pineapple,
  drained
¼ tsp. ground allspice
1 tbsp. lime juice
1 tbsp. sugar
¾ cup dry white wine
salt and pepper to taste

Soak raisins in orange juice. Dredge chicken parts in flour and sauté in oil until browned on all sides. Put chicken in a casserole, combine raisins, orange juice and all other ingredients and pour over chicken. Bake in 325^0 oven for 30 minutes basting frequently. Increase heat to 400^0 and bake 10 more minutes.

Chicken Granada
(for 6)

3 lbs. chicken pieces
(breasts and thighs)
2 tsp. paprika
2 tsp. garlic salt
2 tsp. celery salt
1 cup rice

1½ cups hot chicken broth
2 tsp. lemon juice
½ tsp. tabasco sauce
2 tbsp. parsley, chopped
salt and pepper to taste
⅓ cup sliced stuffed
Spanish olives

Season chicken pieces with paprika, garlic and celery salts. Put in a shallow casserole and bake, skin side up, in a 425⁰ oven for 20 minutes. Remove chicken from casserole, add all other ingredients except olives, mix well, place chicken on top of rice, cover and bake at 350⁰ for 30 minutes or until chicken is tender and all liquid is absorbed. Garnish with sliced olives.

Chicken Granada.→

Zarzuela — See pages 62-63 for recipe.→

Basque Chicken
(for 4)

1 tbsp. butter
3 tbsp. olive oil
1 frying chicken
¼ lb. fresh mushrooms, sliced
1 medium onion, chopped
2 cans (8 oz. each) tomato
   sauce
½ cup dry white wine
10 small white whole
   onions, peeled

2 sprigs parsley
1 clove garlic, minced
salt and pepper to taste
½ cup small pimiento-
   stuffed green olives
1 green pepper, cut
   in strips
2 medium ripe tomatoes, peeled
   and cut into wedges
hot cooked rice

Heat butter and 2 tablespoons olive oil in a heavy casserole. Truss and fry the chicken on all sides until golden brown. Remove from pan. Sauté mushrooms, onion and garlic in the same pan until light brown. Add tomato sauce, wine, whole onions, parsley. Return chicken to pan, sprinkle with salt and pepper. Cover and simmer for about 1 hour or until chicken is tender, basting the chicken occasionally with the sauce. Add olives for the last 15 minutes of cooking time. When done, place chicken on a platter and keep warm. Simmer sauce uncovered for 5 minutes. Heat 1 tablespoon oil in a small skillet, sauté green pepper strips for 2 minutes, add tomato wedges and cook until hot. Arrange on platter around the chicken. Using a slotted spoon lift mushrooms, onions and olives from the sauce and arrange on the platter. Serve with the sauce and rice.

←*Basque Chicken.*

←*Shrimp Ajillo* and *Strawberry Cake Jerez* — See pages 31 and 143 for recipes.

Mexican Chicken
(for 6)

1 frying chicken (3 lbs.)
  cut in 6 pieces
⅓ cup flour
2 tbsp. oil
2 tbsp. butter
½ lb. cooked ham, cut
  into thin slivers
1 cup dark seedless raisins
salt and pepper to taste

⅛ tsp. ground cloves
¼ tsp. ground cumin
2 cloves garlic, crushed
1 cup dry white wine
1 cup chicken broth
½ cup pimiento-stuffed
  olives, halved
1 tbsp. capers, drained
½ cup toasted slivered
  almonds

Shake chicken with flour in a large paper bag. Heat oil and butter in a heavy casserole over medium heat. Fry chicken pieces until golden brown. Pour off excess fat, sprinkle ham and raisins over chicken. Combine salt, pepper, cloves, cumin, garlic, wine and chicken broth. Pour over chicken, cover and simmer for about 1 hour or until chicken is tender. Add olives and capers, cook uncovered to heat through. Sprinkle almonds on top just before serving.

Chicken Pepitoria

(for 6)

1 frying chicken (3 lbs.)
   cut in pieces
4 tbsp. olive oil
2 cloves garlic
1 onion, sliced
1 cup dry white wine
1 tbsp. flour
2 cups chicken broth
salt and pepper to taste

1 bay leaf
pinch of thyme
12 blanched almonds, chopped
¼ tsp. Spanish saffron
2 hard-boiled eggs, chopped
½ cup white soft breadcrumbs,
   sautéed in butter to brown
1 tbsp. parsley, minced

Sauté chicken pieces in oil until golden brown. Add garlic and onion, fry another minute or so, add wine, stir and cook until the wine is reduced to half. Stir in flour, blend well, then add the chicken broth, bay leaf and thyme, salt and pepper. The liquid should just about cover the chicken pieces. Cover pan and cook gently for half an hour. Then add almonds and saffron, stir well, cover and cook until chicken is tender, about another half hour. Just before serving, sprinkle with chopped egg, fried breadcrumbs, and parsley.

Turkey Mole
(for 8)

1 small young turkey
  (about 7 lbs.)

For the sauce:

4 large tomatoes, peeled
  and seeded
2 green peppers, seeded
  and chopped
4 cloves garlic, chopped
1 fried stale tortilla
  (or 1 slice white toast)
½ cup blanched almonds
¼ cup raisins
¼ cup peanuts

1 tbsp. salt
⅓ cup olive oil
1 onion stuck with 2 cloves

2 tbsp. sesame seed
½ tsp. coriander seed
½ tsp. anise seed
¼ tsp. ground cinnamon
¼ tsp. allspice
1½ tbsp. chili powder
2 ozs. unsweetened
  chocolate, grated
salt and pepper to taste
2 cups broth

Disjoint turkey and cut into serving pieces. Put the pieces in a saucepan, barely cover with water, add salt and onion stuck with cloves, bring to a boil and cover. Cook gently for about 1 hour, or until bird is nearly cooked. Remove turkey pieces, drain. Reserve 2 cups of the broth.

Heat half the olive oil in a skillet and sauté the turkey pieces until they are browned on all sides.

Put all other ingredients, except oil and stock in a blender and blend at medium speed until a paste is formed. Add a little water if necessary.

Heat the remaining oil, add the chocolate mixture, blend well and simmer for a minute, stirring constantly, add broth and blend well. The sauce should have the consistency of heavy cream. Place turkey pieces in a heavy saucepan, spoon sauce over it and cook gently for another hour or so.

Turkey Casserole
(for 6)

1 small young turkey
(about 6 lbs.) cut in
  serving pieces
1 tbsp. paprika
2 large cloves garlic,
  crushed
salt and coarsely ground
  pepper to taste
1 tsp. dijon mustard
½ cup wine vinegar
2 tbsp. lemon juice

2 bay leaves
4 tbsp. olive oil
4 tbsp. butter
½ cup chopped onions
2 cups chicken broth
2 green peppers, seeded
  and sliced
¼ cup canned pimientos,
  sliced
12 large pitted olives,
  sliced

Place the turkey pieces in a bowl. Blend paprika, garlic, salt and pepper, mustard and lemon juice and rub this mixture into the turkey pieces. Add vinegar and bay leaves, mix again and let stand for two or three hours. Then drain the turkey, sauté in combined oil and butter until golden brown on all sides, add onions, stir and sauté 2 or 3 minutes longer. Add chicken broth, cover and cook slowly for about 2 hours or until meat is tender. Add all other ingredients and simmer 15 more minutes.

Turkey Terrine
(for 4)

3 cups cooked turkey meat,
  ground
4 to 5 slices firm white
  stale bread
2 eggs
2 tbsp. grated onion
1 tbsp. parsley, minced
salt and pepper to taste
¼ tsp. allspice

½ tsp. coriander, ground
2 tsp. paprika
6 cups chicken broth (or
  turkey broth made from the
  carcass)
¼ cup dry sherry
1 green pepper, seeded and
  diced small
2 scallions, minced

Soak bread in some of the broth, squeeze dry. Blend turkey meat with bread, eggs, onions and all seasonings. Shape mixture into small balls. Mix chicken broth and sherry, bring to a simmer. Put turkey balls gently into the broth and simmer for about 20 minutes. Remove them with a slotted spoon and keep warm. Reduce broth by about one third, return turkey balls to the broth, add the peppers and scallions and simmer another 10 minutes.

Stuffed Flank Steak

(for 4)

4 chorizo sausages
  (about ½ lb.)
1 small onion, minced
¼ cup green olives, chopped
1 tbsp. chili powder
¼ cup minced parsley
1 egg, beaten
½ cup breadcrumbs
salt to taste
½ tsp. oregano

1 flank steak (about 2½ lbs.)
1 clove garlic, crushed
1 tsp. salt
flour
3 tbsp. oil
½ cup beef broth
1 cup tomato sauce (canned)
½ cup dry red wine
1 small bay leaf

Remove casing from sausages, break up the meat and mix with onion, olives, chili powder, parsley, egg, breadcrumbs and salt.

Flatten flank steak with a mallet or ask your butcher to do it. Combine garlic and salt and rub steak on both sides with the mixture. Spread the sausage mixture on the steak, roll it up and fasten it with string or skewers. Dredge with flour and sauté in a heavy saucepan until browned on all sides. Pour off the oil, mix all other ingredients, add to pan, cover and cook in 350⁰ oven for 1½ hours or until meat is soft.

Ropa Vieja

(for 4)

1 flank steak (1 ½ to 2 lbs.)
1 carrot, peeled

1 turnip, quartered
2 cloves

For the sauce:

2 tbsp. lard or oil
1 medium onion, chopped
3 green peppers, seeded
  and chopped
2 cloves garlic, minced
1 tbsp. paprika

3 large tomatoes, peeled,
  seeded and chopped
¼ cup canned pimientos,
  chopped
1 small bay leaf
salt and pepper to taste

Put flank steak in a pan, cover with water, add carrot, turnip and cloves, cover and boil gently until meat is cooked and very soft (2 to 3 hours). Remove meat, drain and shred it with your fingers.

Heat lard in a heavy saucepan, sauté onion until it starts to color, add garlic and peppers, sauté for a couple of minutes. Then add all other ingredients, bring to a boil and simmer for 15 minutes.

Chili Con Carne
(for 8)

6 tbsp. olive oil
3 lbs. lean beef, ground
1 large onion, chopped
1 green pepper, seeded
   and chopped
2 cloves garlic, minced
2 tsp. paprika
3 tbsp. chili powder
1 tsp. oregano
¼ tsp. allspice

salt to taste
4 cups of water
3 cups beef broth
4 cups drained, canned
   tomatoes
2 tbsp. cornstarch
6 tbsp. water
2 cups cooked or canned
   kidney beans

Heat oil in a casserole, brown meat, then add onion, pepper and garlic, mix and sauté another 2 minutes. Add paprika, chili powder, oregano, allspice, salt, water and beef broth, cover and simmer for 45 minutes. Stir occasionally. Add tomatoes, mix and simmer for 30 minutes more. Dilute cornstarch with water, add to meat and blend well and simmer until sauce thickens. Add beans, mix and heat through.

Meat Balls in Almond Sauce
(for 4)

½ lb. lean beef, ground
½ lb. lean pork, ground
2 slices stale bread
milk
1 egg
salt and pepper to taste

½ tsp. oregano
1 tbsp. grated onion
1 tbsp. parsley, minced
salt and pepper to taste
1 recipe almond sauce *(p. 7)*
¾ cup beef broth

Soak the stale bread in milk, squeeze dry and mix with meats. Add all other ingredients except almond sauce and broth, blend well and shape into small balls the size of a walnut.

Mix almond sauce and broth, heat in a saucepan and add the meatballs. Bring to a simmer, cover and cook for about 30 minutes.

Savory Meat Balls

(for 6)

1 lb. ground lean beef
½ lb. ground lean pork
½ lb. ground veal
1 cup cooked rice
¾ cup minced onion
2 cloves garlic, minced

2 tbsp. parsley, minced
½ tsp. dried rosemary,
   crumbled
1 egg
salt and pepper to taste
½ tsp. sage
2 tsp. chili powder

For the Sauce:

1½ tbsp. olive oil
½ cup minced onion
2 cups tomato sauce

1 cup beef broth
1 tbsp. sugar
salt and pepper to taste

Combine all ingredients for the meat balls, and mix well. Then shape the meat mixture into small balls.

For the sauce, heat oil in a heavy casserole, sauté onion until light golden, add tomato sauce, broth, sugar, salt and pepper and bring to a simmer. Add the meatballs, cover and cook gently for about 45 minutes.

Picadillo

(Mexican Hash)
(for 6)

1 lb. ground lean pork
1 lb. ground lean beef
2 tbsp. oil
1 medium onion, chopped
1 clove garlic, chopped
2 tomatoes, peeled, seeded
and chopped
¼ cup beef broth
1 tart green apple, peeled,
cored and grated
1 tbsp. sugar

3 tbsp. blanched almonds,
slivered
3 tbsp. chopped black olives
2 tbsp. chili powder
pinch of cinnamon
pinch of allspice
pinch of cumin
1 tbsp. vinegar
salt and pepper to taste
¼ cup raisins, soaked in
water and drained

Brown meats and onion in oil. Add the tomatoes and beef broth, blend well. When mixture starts to simmer, add all other ingredients, mix well. Bring to a boil and simmer for about 30 minutes. Stir occasionally and add a little more broth if hash gets too dry. Serve with rice or beans.

Roast Leg of Lamb
(for 6)

1 leg of lamb (5 to 6 lbs.)
well trimmed
2 tbsp. olive oil
1½ tsp. chili powder
1½ tsp. oregano
1 tsp. crushed rosemary
1 tsp. crushed caraway seeds
2 cloves garlic, crushed

1 tbsp. paprika
2 tsp. dijon mustard
1 tsp. brown sugar
salt and pepper to taste
2 tbsp. sherry
¼ cup lemon juice
¼ cup olive oil

Combine all ingredients, except lemon juice and ¼ cup olive oil, to make a smooth paste. With a sharp knife make incisions all over the leg of lamb and rub some of the paste into the incisions. Blend lemon juice and olive oil, coat lamb with the mixture, cover and refrigerate for 24 hours. Turn the meat 2 or 3 times while marinating. Remove lamb from refrigerator 3 hours before cooking. Wipe off excess marinade, roast at 350° 15 to 16 minutes per pound for pink, and 20 minutes for well-done meat.

Braised Lamb Shanks
(for 4)

4 lamb shanks
flour
salt and pepper
2 tbsp. oil
½ cup chopped onions
1 large clove garlic, minced
½ cup celery, chopped

⅛ tsp. thyme
¼ tsp. rosemary
1 tbsp. paprika
1 cup tomato sauce
½ cup dry red wine
1 bay leaf
salt and pepper to taste

Trim lamb shanks, dredge with flour, season with salt and pepper and brown over medium heat in oil; add all other ingredients, cover and simmer for about one hour or until meat is tender. Turn and baste the shanks occasionally.

Braised Pork Loin
(for 6)

3 lbs. loin of pork, boned
2 cloves garlic, crushed
2 medium onions, sliced
1 small bay leaf

1 pinch dried rosemary
salt and pepper to taste
¾ cup dry red wine
¼ cup orange juice

Trim pork, remove as much excess fat as possible, tie it to keep its shape. Put onion and garlic in a heavy casserole, place meat on top and add bay leaf and rosemary, sprinkle with salt and pepper and ¼ cup wine. Roast in 350⁰ oven for 30 minutes. Then add remaining wine and orange juice, cover and cook for 1½ hours. Turn meat once or twice while cooking.

Mexican Pork Roast
(for 6 to 8)

center cut loin of pork
(4 lbs.)
½ tsp. thyme
1 tsp. rosemary, crushed
1 tsp. dried marjoram
1 tbsp. paprika
1 large clove garlic, mashed
1 tsp. chili powder

1 tsp. meat extract
(bovril or other)
salt and pepper to taste
1 cup dry white wine
⅓ cup sherry wine
½ cup guava jelly
1½ tbsp. oil

Have butcher bone the loin, remove all fat down to the bare meat. Tie the roast in a roll. Mash garlic with a little salt or through a garlic press, add all herbs, crush and blend them into the garlic paste. Add paprika, oil, chili powder, meat extract, salt and pepper; blend well and rub this mixture into the roast.

Place pork in a roasting pan — do not use a rack — add ½ cup white wine to the pan and put in a preheated 400° oven. After 15 minutes reduce the temperature to 350°. Continue roasting for 25 minutes per pound (weighed after boning and trimming). Baste frequently and add more wine if more basting liquid is needed.

Melt guava jelly over a low flame, combine with sherry wine. 15 minutes before roast is done spread the guava mixture on top of the roast and increase oven temperature to 400°. When done remove roast to hot serving platter and remove strings. Add a little more wine or water to the roasting pan to make a pan gravy.

Serve with plain saffron rice surrounding the roast.

Mexican Pork Roast.→

Chorizos

This sausage, used extensively in all Spanish and Mexican cooking, can be purchased in most Mexican or Latin American food stores. If unavailable, it can be made quite easily at home.

2 lbs. lean pork, ground
6 ounces pork fat, diced
¾ cup minced onion
4 cloves garlic, crushed
4 tbsp. chili powder
⅓ cup canned pimiento, chopped
1 tsp. cinnamon

1 tsp. cumin
1½ tsp. oregano, crushed
1½ tbsp. paprika
½ tsp. coriander, ground
4 tbsp. vinegar
2 tsp. salt
½ tsp. pepper

Blend all ingredients well, let stand for a few hours and mix again. Then fill them into casings, or simply shape into patties and fry. Chorizos can be frozen. Refrigerated they will keep for several weeks. To taste whether they need more seasoning, fry a small patty in a skillet.

←*Cheese Enchiladas* — See page 100 for recipe.

Chorizos and Lentils
(for 4)

8 chorizos (or 1 lb. patties)
1 cup cooked yellow lentils
1 onion, sliced thin
1 clove garlic, minced
1 green pepper, seeded
  and chopped

1 large tomato, peeled,
  seeded and chopped
1 small bay leaf
1 tbsp. wine vinegar
salt and pepper to taste

Fry sausages, or small patties, lightly for about 5 minutes. Remove and reserve. (If sausages are used, cut them into 1 inch rounds). Pour off some of the fat rendered in frying, add the lentils, onion, garlic, and green pepper to pan and fry gently for about 10 minutes, until onions start to take on color. Stir while frying. Add tomatoes and all other ingredients, cover and simmer for 10 to 20 minutes.

Corn is the Mexican staff of life and masa, the Mexican corn flour the mainstay of the Mexican diet. The names of the various corn preparations seem to confuse many people, but it is really quite easy to understand the differences between the various pancake-like items of everyday Mexican cooking.

Tortillas are the basic food, an unleavened bread made from masa or sometimes from wheat flour.

Tacos, the Mexican equivalent of our sandwich, are rolled or folded tortillas with meat or other fillings, and can be fried, baked or just heated up.

Enchiladas are tortillas lightly fried, rolled around a filling of meats or other foods, baked in a sauce or fried and dipped in a sauce.

Tostadas are open faced crisp fried tortillas covered with a variety of sauces and foods.

Tamales are made by spreading a masa dough on corn husks. They are then wrapped around savory fillings, tied and steamed.

Corn Tortillas

(about 16 tortillas)

2 cups masa harina (corn flour)
1¼ cups warm water
1 tsp. salt

Combine masa and salt in a bowl, add water and mix well until dough holds together in a ball. Don't use too much water, the dough should not be sticky. Let dough rest for half an hour. The best way to shape tortillas is still the old way — by hand. Divide the dough in 16 pieces and shape each into a ball. Then pat them between the palms of your hands until the flat tortilla is formed. This, however, sounds easier than it is. Probably the easiest method is to put the balls of dough on wax paper or a moist cloth, flatten them slightly with your hand, cover with wax paper or cloth and roll them to the desired thickness. They should be about 6 inches in diameter. Trim evenly before cooking.

To cook tortillas: Heat a soap stone griddle or a cast iron skillet, not greased, over medium heat and cook tortillas for about 2 minutes on each side. They should be still soft and lightly flecked with brown.

Many food stores across the country carry Mexican or Southwestern specialties and it is not all too difficult to find pre-packaged tortillas and tamales. Instant masa flour can also be found in most places or ordered through your grocer. With masa flour it is quite easy to make them.

Tacos with Meat Filling
(for 12 tacos)

1 lb. ground lean beef
2 tbsp. oil
½ cup minced onion
½ cup minced green pepper
1 clove garlic, crushed
⅔ cup cooked potato, diced
1 cup drained canned tomato, chopped
salt and pepper to taste
oil for frying

1 tsp. vinegar
1 tsp. sugar
½ tsp. basil
1 tsp. ground coriander
1 tbsp. chili powder
¼ cup blanched almonds, slivered
¼ cup pitted green olives, chopped
12 tortillas

Fry meat and onions in oil until lightly browned; add pepper and cook until peppers are soft. Add potato, tomatoes, garlic, vinegar, sugar, basil, coriander, chili powder, salt and pepper, mix well and simmer for 10 minutes. Then add almonds and olives and simmer for 10 minutes more. Heat the tortillas to soften, spread some of the mixture on each tortilla, roll up and fasten with toothpicks. Fry in hot oil until they are crisp. Serve with a lettuce and tomato salad and sliced avocados.

Tacos with Turkey Filling

(for 10 tacos)

¼ cup minced onion
¼ cup green peppers, chopped
1 clove garlic, minced
1 tbsp. butter
1 tbsp. chili powder
salt and pepper to taste

½ cup pimiento-stuffed
   green olives, chopped
2 cups cooked turkey meat
   (or chicken)
1 small tomato, peeled,
   seeded and chopped
10 tortillas

Sauté onion, peppers and garlic in butter until soft. Add chili powder, salt, pepper and olives, stir to blend. Add turkey meat and tomato, stir and simmer to heat through. Heat tortillas to soften them, spread with the filling, roll them up and fasten with toothpicks. Fry tortillas in hot oil until crisp.

Baked Tacos
(for 12 tacos)

½ lb. pork, ground
½ lb. beef, ground
4 tbsp. oil
½ cup chopped onion
1 green pepper, seeded
and chopped
1 clove garlic, minced
2 anchovy filets, mashed
2 cups canned tomatoes,
drained and chopped

1 tbsp. raisins
¼ tsp. oregano
1 tsp. chili powder
pinch of cayenne pepper
¾ cup beef broth
12 tortillas
¼ cup parmesan cheese,
grated
¼ cup cheddar cheese, grated
salt and pepper to taste

Heat oil in a skillet, sauté ground pork for a few minutes, stirring occasionally. Add beef and sauté a few minutes longer until meats are lightly browned. Then add ¼ cup chopped onion, half of the chopped pepper, garlic and ¾ cup tomatoes. Blend well, add anchovies, raisins, mix and simmer for 10 minutes.

To make a sauce, combine the rest of the onions, pepper and tomatoes with the oregano, chili powder, cayenne pepper and beef broth. Cook over gentle heat for about half an hour until slightly reduced.

Heat the tortillas to soften them, put part of the meat mixture on each, roll them up and fasten with toothpicks. Arrange in an oiled casserole, spoon the sauce over them and sprinkle with the combined grated cheeses. Season with salt and pepper and bake in a 350° oven for about 20 minutes until the cheese topping is brown.

Cheese Enchiladas
(12 pieces)

1 green pepper, seeded
  and chopped
1 cup tomatoes, peeled, seeded
  and chopped (or drained
  canned tomatoes)
5 scallions, chopped
1 large clove garlic, crushed

salt and pepper to taste
1 tbsp. chili powder
1 cup shortening or lard
1½ cups sharp cheddar
   cheese, chopped
12 tortillas
½ tsp. oregano

Heat 1½ tablespoons shortening in a skillet, sauté pepper and garlic for a couple of minutes, add tomatoes, scallions, oregano, salt, pepper and chili powder, mix well and simmer for 15 minutes. Add the cheese, blend and heat through. Heat the tortillas to soften them, put cheese filling on each of them, fold them over once and fasten with toothpicks. Fry in hot shortening to brown on both sides. Serve a lettuce and tomato salad, or sliced avocados as a garnish.

Chorizo Enchiladas

(for 12 tortillas)

1 lb. chorizos
1 green pepper, seeded
  and chopped
½ cup minced onion

24 pitted black olives
3 cups chili sauce *(p. 9)*
12 tortillas
lard for frying

    Strip sausages out of casing, break up meat with a fork and sauté without added fat for a few minutes, until the meat starts to brown. Fry tortillas for a few moments in hot lard, then spread them with chili sauce. On each tortilla spread a pat of sausage meat, sprinkle with green pepper and onion and place two olives on top. Roll up and place tortillas in a buttered casserole. Cover with remaining sauce and heat in the oven before serving.

Rice

Rice is the mainstay of the Spanish diet and is equally beloved in all Latin American countries. Next to corn, it is the most used staple in Mexico too. Rice is mostly used in combination with a great variety of other foods: seafood, poultry, meats and vegetables. Cooking rice the Spanish way requires a good long-grain rice. The typical way rice is prepared in Spain consists of slightly sautéeing first the meats or vegetables that go into a dish, then adding the dry rice, sautéeing gently until the grain becomes slightly transparent and covered with oil. Only then is the cooking liquid added, and the mixture brought to a full boil for 3 or 4 minutes. Simmering for another 15 minutes or so will cook the rice to perfection. A few drops of lemon juice added to the water or broth used in cooking the rice will help to separate the grains.

The classic and best known rice dishes of Spain — the various Paellas — take their names from the pan they are traditionally prepared and served in, the "paella". It is a flat, round or oval iron pan with two handles. A skillet can be used quite well instead.

Arroz con Pollo
(for 4)

⅓ cup olive oil
1 frying chicken (3 lbs.)
   cut into serving pieces
1 clove garlic, minced
4 scallions, chopped
1 tomato, peeled, seeded
   and chopped

½ cup green pepper, chopped
1 small can pimientos,
   drained and chopped
⅛ tsp. Spanish saffron
1 cup rice
2 cups chicken broth
salt and pepper to taste

Heat oil and sauté chicken until golden brown on all sides. Add garlic and scallions, sauté a few minutes longer, then add rice and sauté over gentle heat, stirring often, until all grains are coated with oil and somewhat transparent. Dissolve saffron in a little broth and add, together with all other ingredients, to pan. Blend well, cover and simmer for about 20 minutes until rice is done and all liquid absorbed.

Farmer's Paella
(for 6)

½ lb. smoked ham, sliced
1 frying chicken, cut up and parboiled for 10 minutes
½ lb. lean boneless lamb, cubed
¼ lb. chorizos, sliced
1 small onion, sliced

1 bay leaf
¼ tsp. Spanish saffron
½ tsp. crushed red pepper
2 cups rice, washed
6 to 8 cups chicken broth
salt and pepper to taste
3 cloves garlic, sliced

Put all ingredients with 6 cups chicken broth in a deep saucepan, mix and distribute well, bring to a boil and then cook uncovered, stirring from time to time to prevent food from sticking. Add more broth as the liquid evaporates. When rice is just about cooked, put casserole in a 350⁰ oven to dry out and finish cooking.

Rice with Chicken Livers
(for 4)

½ lb. chicken livers
2 tbsp. butter
salt and pepper to taste
4 tbsp. olive oil
⅔ cup minced onion
1 clove garlic, minced
1½ cups rice

3 cups chicken broth
¾ cup tomato sauce
½ tsp. oregano
½ tsp. marjoram
1 tsp. vinegar
3 tbsp. parsley, minced
pinch of cayenne pepper

Sauté chicken livers in butter for about 3 minutes until they are browned but still a little pink inside. Season with salt and pepper, chop coarsely and keep warm.

Heat oil in a heavy casserole, add onion and garlic and sauté until soft. Then add rice, stir to coat all grains with oil and sauté, stirring, until rice is translucent and just starts to take on color. Heat broth and tomato sauce, add to rice, bring to a boil. Add all other ingredients except livers, mix well, cover and cook over medium heat for 10 minutes. Stir with a fork, cover again and cook over gentle heat another 10 minutes or until liquid has been nearly absorbed. Mix in chicken livers, cover and simmer until rice is dry and cooked. If needed, add more broth during cooking.

Clams and Rice
(for 4)

2 dozen small clams (or 1
   cup canned whole
   baby clams, drained)
$2/3$ cup onion, minced
2 cloves garlic, minced
3 tbsp. olive oil
1½ cups rice
1 tbsp. parsley, minced

1 large green or red sweet
   pepper, seeded and diced
¼ tsp. Spanish saffron
3 cups liquid (clam
   juice and chicken
   broth combined)
salt and pepper to taste

Steam clams open, cut them in half and reserve. Strain and reserve broth.

Heat oil in a heavy pan, sauté onion and garlic until soft, add rice and stir until coated with oil and rice is translucent and starting to turn yellow. Add diced pepper, clams, mix; add liquid, saffron and salt and pepper. Bring to a boil, cover and cook gently for 10 minutes. Stir with a fork, blend in parsley, cover again and cook another 15 minutes or until liquid has been absorbed and rice is cooked.

Rice and Shrimp
(for 4)

1 lb. medium shrimp, peeled and deveined
1½ cups rice
⅔ cup minced onion
3 cloves garlic, minced
3 tbsp. olive oil

1 cup tomatoes, peeled, seeded and chopped
1 tsp. paprika
salt and pepper to taste
1½ cups chicken broth
1½ cups water

Heat oil in a heavy casserole, add onion and garlic, sauté until soft but do not brown. Add rice, stir to coat with oil and sauté while stirring until rice is translucent and starts to turn yellow. Add tomatoes, stir and sauté gently for another minute. Add paprika, hot chicken broth and ¾ cup water, shrimps, salt and pepper. Mix well, bring to a boil, cover and cook over gentle heat for about 20 minutes or until liquid is absorbed and rice is cooked. Add more water during cooking if necessary.

Paella
(for 6)

¼ cup olive oil
1 frying chicken (2½ lbs)
   cut in pieces
1 lb. chorizo sausages, parboiled and cut in 1 inch
   pieces
¾ cup onion, chopped
2 cloves garlic, crushed
1½ cups rice
2 cups chicken broth
2 cans (5 oz. each) whole
   baby clams

¼ tsp. Spanish saffron
salt and pepper to taste
1 package frozen artichoke
   hearts, partially thawed
2 ripe tomatoes, peeled and
   cut in thin wedges
1 cup small whole
   pimiento-stuffed green
   Spanish olives
1 lb. shrimp, peeled, deveined,
   and cooked for about
   3 minutes

Heat oil in a 4-quart paella pan or a 13-inch skillet. Add chicken and chorizos and sauté until chicken is browned on all sides. Remove chicken and sausage and pour off all but 2 tablespoons of the fat. Add onion and garlic, sauté until soft, then add rice and sauté over gentle heat for about 2 or 3 minutes until rice is coated with oil and transparent. Stir constantly. Add chicken broth, the juice from the clams, the saffron, salt and pepper. Bring to a boil, stir well and return chicken and chorizos to pan, stir and simmer for about 25 minutes, stirring occasionally. If needed, add more broth to prevent sticking.

Stir in artichoke hearts, olives and tomatoes, cook for 5 minutes, then add shrimp and drained clams, stir and cook for 5 more minutes until all ingredients are hot.

Paella.→

Rice with Pork and Sour Cream
(for 4)

1½ lbs. lean boneless pork (loin or tenderloin)
1 tbsp. oil
1 tbsp. butter
½ cup chopped onion
1 clove garlic, crushed

1 tsp. paprika
¼ tsp. rosemary leaves, crushed
2 tbsp. parsley, minced
2½ cups hot beef broth
1 cup sour cream
salt and pepper to taste

Cut pork into small cubes, heat butter and oil in a heavy casserole, add meat and brown well. Pour off all but 2 tablespoons of fat, add onion and garlic, stir and sauté for 2 or 3 minutes.

Add paprika, rosemary, parsley and broth, season with salt and pepper, cover and simmer for 15 minutes. Stir in rice, bring to a rapid boil, reduce heat, cover and cook for 15 minutes. Blend in sour cream, correct seasoning, cover and cook gently for another 10 minutes or until rice is cooked.

←*Tacos with Meat Filling* — See page 97 for recipe.

Rice and Vegetables
(for 4)

1½ cups rice
3 tbsp. olive oil
1 medium onion, chopped
1 clove garlic, minced
1 large tomato, peeled,
  seeded and chopped
3 cups chicken broth

1 green pepper, seeded
  and chopped
1 green chili pepper, minced
½ tsp. marjoram
½ tsp. oregano
2 tsp. chili powder
salt to taste

Heat olive oil in a saucepan, add onion and garlic and sauté until they just start to color; add rice, sauté while stirring until rice is well coated with oil and translucent. Add all vegetables and seasonings, stir and sauté another minute or so, then add hot chicken broth, mix and bring to a boil. Cover and cook over medium heat for 10 minutes, then lower heat to simmer, stir once with a fork and continue cooking until all liquid has been absorbed and rice is cooked. Add a little more broth if necessary.

Beans — frijoles — are another of the very important items in the Spanish/Mexican diet. They are served in many ways, as appetizer, as vegetable, or as main dish.

Basic Recipe for Beans
(for 6)

2 cups pinto or red beans   salt to taste
1½ qts. water   ½ cup or more lard

    Soak beans overnight with water to cover. Some of the water will have been absorbed by morning — add more to cover. Add salt and cook slowly for about 2 hours or until very tender. Mash well and add the melted hot lard gradually, while still cooking the beans. Stir while adding the lard, to prevent sticking. If available, use bacon fat instead of lard, it improves the flavor.

    If using canned beans, drain the can, mash the beans. Heat ¼ cup lard in a skillet, stir in the mashed beans and add the liquid from the can, a little at a time, until well blended.

Frijoles Refritos
(Refried Beans)

Heat lard or bacon drippings in a skillet, add some minced onion and sauté lightly. Then add mashed beans as prepared in the basic recipe for beans, and fry, stirring, until the beans are dry. Use ample fat for preparing refried beans.

Refried beans can be used as a base for a variety of casserole dishes. In combination with fried chorizos; with various toppings; they can be scrambled with eggs and peppers or chilis; and of course, used as filling for tortillas, tostadas and sandwiches.

Refried Beans and Tomato

(for 4)

3 cups basic mashed beans
5 tbsp. lard or bacon drippings
1 small onion, minced

1 clove garlic, minced
8 tbsp. tomato paste
1 tbsp. chili powder

Heat lard in a skillet, sauté onion and garlic until light golden. Add the beans and stir well, then add tomato paste and chili powder, blend and heat through while stirring.

Refried Beans and Cheese
(for 4)

3 cups basic mashed beans $^2/_3$ cup cheddar cheese,
5 tbsp. lard or bacon drippings   cubed

Heat lard in a skillet, add beans and proceed as in making Frijoles Refritos. After cooking and stirring the beans for a few minutes, add the cubed cheese, let it melt and serve.

Beans in a Pot

(Frijoles de Olla)
(for 8)

2 cups kidney or pinto beans
½ lb. lean salt pork, diced
¼ lb. smoked ham, diced
2 cloves garlic, minced

chili sauce *(p. 9)* to taste
1 large Spanish onion, sliced thin
$1/_3$ cup grated parmesan cheese
$1/_3$ cup grated cheddar cheese
salt to taste

    Soak beans overnight in cold water. Drain and cover with cold water. Bring to a boil, add salt pork, ham and garlic, lower heat, cover and simmer for 1½ to 2 hours until beans are cooked. Add more warm water during cooking if necessary. When beans are cooked and all the water absorbed, put them in a serving dish, add chili sauce, blend in gently, salt to taste, top with onion rings and grated cheeses.

Savory Chick Peas
(for 6)

1 lb. dry chick peas
3 rashers bacon
1 small onion, minced
1 clove garlic, minced
1 cup tomato sauce
½ cup dry white wine
1 tbsp. chili powder

1 tsp. powdered cumin
1½ tbsp. parsley, chopped
1 cup chicken broth
water
3 chorizo sausages,
   fried and sliced
salt and pepper to taste

Soak chick peas overnight in cold water to cover. Drain peas, put them in a casserole, add broth, wine, water to cover. Cover and cook for about one hour until the peas are nearly cooked.

Fry the bacon in another casserole, remove bacon and sauté onion and garlic in bacon drippings until soft; add tomato sauce, chili powder, cumin and parsley, simmer for 5 minutes. Then add the chick peas along with the liquid they cooked in, the sliced sausages and the crumbled bacon. Season with salt and pepper and cook uncovered until the sauce has thickened.

Creamed Chick Peas

(for 4)

3 tbsp. lard (or bacon
  drippings)
½ cup minced onion
1 clove garlic, minced
1½ tbsp. flour
1½ cups canned chick peas

⅓ cup chicken broth (or water)
1 tbsp. chili powder
salt and pepper to taste
2 hot Italian sausages,
  fried and diced

Heat fat in a heavy skillet, add onion and garlic and sauté until soft but not browned. Add flour, sauté while stirring until flour starts to color, then add the chick peas and the liquid from the can, season with salt and pepper and cook for about 10 minutes. Force contents of the skillet through a sieve or strainer and return to skillet. Add chicken broth, blend and cook, whipping occasionally with a whisk until the peas are creamy and light. Blend in chili powder, cook for another few minutes and mix in the fried sausage just before serving.

Chick Peas in Tomato Sauce
(for 6)

1 lb. dried chick peas
3 cups chicken broth
3 cups water
1 medium onion, minced
2 cloves garlic, minced
1 tbsp. paprika
salt and pepper to taste

½ tsp. marjoram
⅓ cup olive oil
2 cups canned tomatoes
 (measured drained)
½ cup canned pimientos,
 cut in strips
1 tbsp. parsley, chopped

Soak chick peas overnight in cold water to cover. Drain, put in a saucepan, add broth, water, onion, garlic, paprika, salt, pepper, marjoram and oil. Cover and cook over medium heat for about one hour. Add the tomatoes, mix gently and cook until the chick peas are soft. A few minutes before serving blend in pimientos and parsley.

Lima Bean Casserole

(for 4)

3 tbsp. olive oil
1 medium onion, minced
2 cloves garlic, minced
½ cup smoked ham, diced
2 cups fresh shelled
    lima beans

2 Italian sausages,
    fried and sliced
1 tbsp. parsley, minced
1 cup dry white wine
salt and pepper to taste

Heat oil in a casserole, add onion and garlic and sauté for a few minutes until soft. Add ham and sliced sausages, stir and sauté about 5 minutes longer. Blend in all other ingredients, cover and simmer for 45 minutes or until beans are cooked.

Mushrooms and Sour Cream
(for 4)

1 lb. firm button mushrooms	2 tbsp. chili powder
2 tbsp. olive oil	1 tsp. paprika
1 tbsp. butter	2 tsp. flour
1 tbsp. parsley, chopped	salt and pepper to taste
1 clove garlic, minced	½ cup sour cream

Trim mushrooms. Heat oil and butter in a skillet, add garlic and sauté for a few seconds, add mushrooms, parsley, chili powder, paprika, blend and sauté for a few minutes until mushrooms are just done — do not overcook. Stir in flour and sauté 2 more minutes, season with salt and pepper and stir in sour cream. Blend well and heat through and serve.

Fried Plantains
(for 4)

2 plantains (cooking bananas)
  or under-ripe bananas
¼ cup lemon juice
3 eggs
¼ cup flour

3 tbsp. milk
½ tsp. salt
⅛ tsp. pepper
½ tsp. chili powder
oil for frying

Peel plantains and cut lengthwise in half. Brush each half with lemon juice.

Prepare batter: beat egg yolks until creamy, beat egg whites stiff. Mix flour, salt, pepper, chili powder with the egg yolks, fold in egg whites.

Put oil about 1 inch deep in a heavy skillet, heat over medium flame. Coat plantain halves with batter and fry them, two at a time until browned on both sides. Drain and serve.

Spinach and Pimiento
(for 4)

2 lbs. spinach
4 tbsp. olive oil
2 cloves garlic, crushed
1 tbsp. flour
1 tbsp. butter
$1/3$ cup light cream

pinch of grated nutmeg
1 tsp. chili powder
1 tsp. lemon juice
hard-boiled eggs, sliced
canned pimientos, cut
   in strips

Wash spinach well, drain, trim off coarse stems. Heat oil in a saucepan, add garlic, sauté for a few seconds, add spinach and cook while stirring until the leaves are well wilted. Drain again and chop spinach quite fine.

Heat butter in a saucepan, stir in flour and sauté while stirring for a couple of minutes. Do not let the roux brown. Then add gradually the cream, stir until mixture thickens and is smooth. Blend in nutmeg, chili powder and lemon juice, then add spinach and mix well. Stir until spinach is hot. Before serving garnish the top with egg slices and pimiento.

Squash Pancakes
(for 4)

2 cups raw, yellow summer
squash or zucchini,
peeled and grated
½ cup flour
1 tsp. baking powder

1 tbsp. parsley, minced
1 tbsp. grated onion
salt and pepper to taste
butter
1 tsp. lemon juice

Sift flour and baking powder over grated squash, blend; mix in lemon juice, onion, parsley, salt and pepper. Heat butter in skillet and fry the mixture as you would pancakes, making about 8 small pancakes.

Mexican Succotash
(Colache)
(for 6)

¼ cup butter
1 lb. zucchini, sliced
½ cup chopped onion
1 green pepper,
   seeded and diced
¼ cup canned pimiento, diced

2 large tomatoes, peeled,
   seeded and coarsely chopped
1½ cups fresh corn,
   cut off the cob
salt and pepper to taste

    Sauté onion in butter until light golden, add all vegetables, salt and pepper, cover and simmer until vegetables are tender. If liquid is needed during cooking, add a little chicken broth or water.

Vegetable Stew
(for 6)

2 tbsp. butter
²/₃ cup minced onion
2 cloves garlic, crushed
½ cup tomato sauce
½ cup chicken broth
1½ cups potatoes, diced
   small
2 zucchini, peeled and diced
½ cup grated parmesan
   cheese

1 cup fresh corn,
   cut off the cob
1 cup green peas, shelled
½ cup firm button
   mushrooms
1 green chili pepper, chopped
1 tbsp. paprika
1 tsp. oregano
salt and pepper to taste

Heat butter in a casserole, add onion and garlic and sauté until light golden brown. Add tomato sauce, chicken broth, and potatoes and simmer for 5 minutes. Then add all other ingredients except cheese, cover and simmer gently for about 45 minutes. Just before serving stir in cheese and heat through once more.

Mexican Corn

(for 4)

1½ cups fresh sweet corn,
  cut from cob
2 medium ripe tomatoes,
  peeled, seeded and
  chopped
½ cup chopped green pepper
3 tbsp. minced onion
2 tbsp. butter

1 tbsp. flour
1 tbsp. chili powder
salt and pepper to taste
1 cup sharp cheddar
  cheese, grated
½ cup pitted ripe
  olives, sliced

Heat butter and sauté onion and pepper until tender. Add flour, chili powder, salt and pepper, stir and simmer for a minute. Add corn, tomatoes, bring to a simmer and cook for a few minutes until the corn is done. Add a little water if mixture is too dry. Stir in grated cheese and olives, stir and heat until cheese melts and serve.

Stuffed Avocado

(for 4)

2 ripe avocados
2 tbsp. lemon juice
²/₃ cup cooked ham, minced
1 tbsp. grated onion
1 tbsp. parsley, minced
canned pimiento,
   cut in strips

¼ cup canned pimientos,
   chopped
²/₃ cup mayonnaise
salt and pepper to taste
1 hard-boiled egg,
   quartered

Peel avocados, cut in half lengthwise and remove pit. Brush the surface of each half with lemon juice. Combine ham, onion, parsley, chopped pimiento and mayonnaise, blend well, season with salt and pepper and fill the avocado cavities, mounding the filling. Garnish the top of each half with egg and pimiento strips.

Avocado with Tomato Stuffing
(for 4)

2 large avocados
2 tbsp. lemon juice
2 firm ripe tomatoes, peeled,
    seeded and diced
4 scallions, minced
4 tbsp. olive oil
1½ tbsp. vinegar
1 tsp. sugar

salt and pepper to taste
½ tsp. basil
2 tbsp. chopped green olives
pinch of cayenne pepper
mayonnaise
crisp romaine lettuce
    leaves

Peel the avocados, cut in half lengthwise, and remove pit. Brush the surfaces with lemon juice. Blend oil, vinegar, sugar, salt, pepper, cayenne and basil. Combine tomatoes, scallions, the dressing and olives, blend well and fill the avocados with the mixture. Coat the mixture with mayonnaise and serve the avocados on crisp leaves of romaine lettuce.

Bean Salad
(for 6)

1 can red kidney beans, drained

1½ tbsp. minced onion

1 cup celery, white part only, chopped

1 tbsp. capers, drained and chopped

2 anchovies, chopped

¼ cup oil

3 tbsp. wine vinegar

½ tsp. oregano

1 tsp. sugar

½ clove garlic, crushed

Blend all ingredients and chill well.

String Bean Salad
(for 4 to 6)

1 lb. string beans
2 small ripe tomatoes,
  cut in wedges
1 small onion, thinly sliced
¼ cup olive oil
3 tbsp. wine vinegar

1 tsp. dijon mustard
salt and pepper to taste
½ tsp. basil
1 avocado, peeled and
  cut into wedges
2 hard-boiled eggs, quartered

Pare and french the string beans, boil in salted water until just cooked but still crisp. Place in a bowl, add tomatoes and onion slices. Combine oil, vinegar, mustard, salt, pepper and basil; blend well, pour over beans and toss gently to coat them well. Garnish with avocado wedges and quartered eggs.

Raw Cauliflower Salad

(for 4)

1 medium head cauliflower
1 small green pepper, seeded
   and chopped
¼ cup canned pimiento,
   drained and chopped
½ cup pitted ripe olives,
   sliced thick

5 tbsp. olive oil
1½ tbsp. wine vinegar
salt and pepper to taste
1 tbsp. capers, drained
   and chopped
1 anchovy filet, mashed
1 small onion, minced

Trim florets off cauliflower and discard stems. Slice florets, combine with pepper, pimiento, olives, and onion. Blend oil, vinegar, salt, pepper, capers and anchovy, pour over cauliflower and mix well. Chill for a few hours before serving.

Avocado Salad Acapulco
(for one person)

¼ cup diced cooked lobster
  meat
¼ cup shredded heart of
  romaine lettuce
1 tsp. capers
2 tbsp. mayonnaise
salt and freshly ground
  pepper

½ large avocado
juice of ½ lemon
1 round slice lobster meat
  from the tail
1 tsp. minced parsley
paprika

Mix the diced lobster with the shredded romaine and the capers, combine the salad with the mayonnaise and season with salt and pepper.

Cut the desired number of avocados lengthwise in half, remove the pits. Fill each cavity with the lobster salad, sprinkle with lemon juice and top with round slice of lobster meat. Sprinkle with chopped parsley and paprika. Serve well chilled.

Avocado Salad Acapulco.→

Cauliflower Salad
(for 4)

1 medium cauliflower
1 tbsp. salt
1 tbsp. lemon juice
¼ cup olive oil
3 tbsp. wine vinegar
1 tsp. dijon mustard
salt and pepper to taste
2 tbsp. chopped parsley

1 tsp. dried chervil
¹/₃ cup cooked ham, minced
1 small avocado,
    peeled and diced
1 tbsp. capers, drained
    and chopped
mayonnaise
paprika

Trim florets off the cauliflower and discard the stems. Boil florets in water with 1 tablespoon salt and lemon juice for about 10 minutes until cooked but still firm. Drain well and cool completely. Blend oil, vinegar, mustard, salt, pepper and chevril. Pour dressing over cauliflower, add all other ingredients except mayonnaise, paprika and parsley, blend well but gently. Mound a portion of the salad on each serving plate, coat each mound with mayonnaise, sprinkle with paprika, and parsley. Chill well before serving.

←*Flan* — See page 142 for recipe.

Chicken and Corn Salad
(for 6)

3 cups cooked chicken,
   diced
2 cups cooked corn kernels
   (canned or fresh)
2 cups tomatoes, peeled,
   seeded and chopped
2 green peppers, seeded
   and chopped
4 scallions, minced

½ cup canned pimientos,
   chopped
1 tbsp. capers, drained
   and chopped
2 cups mayonnaise
salt and pepper to taste
hard-boiled eggs and
   lettuce leaves

Blend all ingredients except eggs and lettuce leaves. Chill for an hour. Arrange in a mound on a serving platter and garnish with lettuce leaves and quartered eggs.

Meat Salad
(for 4)

4 cups of lean cooked
  pork or beef, cut
  in julienne strips
1 onion, sliced paper thin
2 tbsp. capers, drained
  and chopped
2 tbsp. pimiento-stuffed
  green olives, sliced

¼ cup olive oil
3 tbsp. wine vinegar
1 tsp. oregano
1 tsp. dijon mustard
1 anchovy filet, mashed
salt and pepper to taste
2 tbsp. chives, chopped

Arrange meat in a shallow serving bowl, top with the sliced onion, sprinkle with capers, olives and chives. Combine and blend all other ingredients, pour over the meat. Chill well before serving.

Pepper Salad
(for 4)

2 sweet green peppers
2 sweet red peppers
4 tbsp. oil
2 tbsp. wine vinegar
salt and pepper to taste

1 tsp. sugar
1 medium onion, sliced paper thin
1 clove garlic, crushed to
   a paste with a little salt

Cut peppers in half, remove membrane and seeds. Parboil in boiling water for about 2 minutes. Drain and cool under cold running water. The peppers should be still firm and crunchy. Cut them into slices. Blend oil, vinegar, salt, pepper and sugar. Put peppers in a serving bowl, add all ingredients and blend well. Chill before serving.

Mexican Shrimp Salad

(for 6)

1 lb. medium shrimp, cooked, shelled and deveined

1½ cups potatoes, cooked and diced

4 hard-boiled eggs, chopped

⅓ cup mayonnaise

¼ cup sour cream

½ tsp. chili powder

1 dash tabasco sauce

1 tbsp. parsley, minced

2 anchovy filets, mashed

salt to taste

paprika

Combine shrimp, potatoes and eggs. Blend all other ingredients except paprika. Combine with shrimp, mix gently and chill for several hours. Sprinkle with paprika before serving.

Flan
(for 6)

⅓ cup light brown sugar
3 cups milk
scant ½ cup sugar
6 tbsp. rum (opt.)

pinch of salt
1 tsp. vanilla extract
6 eggs

Put brown sugar in pan the flan is to be baked in, melt the sugar and stir until sugar starts to turn a deeper brown. Swirl the pan to cover the entire surface with the melted sugar. Remove from heat. Beat the eggs until creamy, beat in sugar, then add salt, milk and vanilla, blend well. Pour the mixture into the caramel lined pan, set the pan in a slightly larger one, half filled with hot water. Bake in a 350⁰ oven for about half an hour or more, until the tip of a knife inserted in the custard comes out clean. Remove from the oven and waterbath, cool. When cool, loosen the edges of the custard with a knife or spatula, place a serving platter on top and invert quickly.

Before serving pour warmed rum over the flan and ignite.

Strawberry Cake Jerez

(for 8)

$1/_3$ cup sugar

2 tbsp. cornstarch

$1/_8$ tsp. salt

1 cup milk

2 eggs

2 cups heavy cream

¾ cup cream sherry

2 pints strawberries

2 packages (3 oz. each)
    plain ladyfingers, split

In a saucepan mix together sugar, cornstarch and salt; gradually stir in milk. Cook over low heat, stirring constantly, until the mixture thickens and starts to simmer. Remove from heat. Beat eggs with 1 cup of heavy cream and stir into milk mixture. Blend well. Cook this mixture over very low heat, stirring constantly, until mixture thickens (about 5 minutes). Do not let boil. Remove from heat and stir in ¼ cup of sherry. Cover and cool thoroughly. Meanwhile wash and hull berries. Save 12 for garnish, slice the remainder, and reserve.

Place half the ladyfingers in a 2½ quart serving bowl, sprinkle with ¼ cup of sherry. Top with half of the sliced berries, then with half the custard. Repeat layers, cover and chill well. Whip remaining cream stiff; spread over the top of the cake. Garnish with whole berries.

Almond Candy
(2 dozen)

1½ cups blanched almonds, ground
¾ cup fine sugar
½ tsp. vanilla

½ tsp. grated lemon rind
2 tbsp. brandy or rum
2 egg whites, stiffly beaten

Blend almonds, sugar, vanilla, lemon rind and brandy. Fold in beaten egg whites. Form into about 2 dozen small balls, put on a buttered baking sheet and bake in 350⁰ oven for about 5 minutes.

Baked Apples
(for 4)

¼ cup flour

¼ cup sugar

¼ cup butter

¼ tsp. cinnamon

⅛ tsp. mace

pinch of salt

4 large firm apples,
   peeled and cored

4 tbsp. rum

⅓ cup orange juice

1 tbsp. lemon juice

¼ cup water

Mix flour, sugar, butter, cinnamon, mace and salt, blend with fingers until crumbly. Fill the apples with the mixture, reserving a little to be sprinkled over the top. Add 1 tablespoon rum to each apple. Put apples in a buttered baking dish, mix orange juice, lemon juice and water and add to dish. Bake at 375⁰ for about 45 minutes or until apples are cooked.

If desired, serve hot apples with whipped cream.

Candied Grapefruit Peel

3 large, thick-skinned
  grapefruit
2½ cups sugar

1½ cups water
granulated sugar

Peel grapefruit and pare off the white part inside the skin. Cut the peel into even strips, about ¼ inch wide and 3 inches long. Place strips into a saucepan and pour boiling water over them to cover. Bring to a boil again, and boil, uncovered, for 5 minutes. Drain and repeat this procedure 4 more times.

Put 2½ cups sugar and 1½ cups water in a pan, bring to a boil and boil for 10 minutes; then add the grapefruit peel and simmer, lightly covered, for about one hour until nearly all the syrup has been absorbed.

Remove strips with a slotted spoon and arrange on a piece of aluminum foil. When they are cool and almost dry, roll them in granulated sugar, let them dry completely and then store in a tight container.

Orange peel can be prepared the same way, but be sure to use thick-skinned fruit.

Baked Bananas
(for 6)

6 ripe unblemished bananas
1 cup sugar
1 cup rum

Make a cut with a sharp knife down the length of each banana so that the skin can be removed in one piece. Carefully take the bananas out of their skin without breaking them. Reserve the skins.

Put the bananas in a deep dish, sprinkle with sugar and pour the rum over them. Let stand for about 3 hours, turning once. Drain bananas, reserving the rum, and put them carefully back into their skins. Tie the skins with a string so that they will not open while baking. Put bananas side by side in a buttered baking dish. Pour the rum over them and bake in a preheated 375^0 oven for about 15 minutes. Remove the string and serve immediately.

Broiled Bananas
(for 6)

6 bananas

½ cup butter, melted

½ cup sugar

½ cup hot rum

Peel the bananas, put them in a baking dish, brush them with melted butter and broil under a medium flame for about 6 to 7 minutes until they are golden brown. Sprinkle with sugar 2 minutes before they are done. Remove from the broiler, pour rum over them, ignite and serve immediately.

Mango Puree

(for 6)

3 large ripe mangos
1½ tbsp. lemon juice
½ cup sugar
   (or to taste)
2 large ripe firm peaches

4 tbsp. light rum
1 cup heavy cream
½ cup slivered blanched
   almonds

Peel and slice mangoes, press through a sieve, add sugar and lemon juice, blend. Peel peaches and cut them in smallish cubes and add to mangoes. Whip cream, fold in almonds and rum and blend with mangoes. Serve in individual cups or in pastry shells. Chill well before serving. Top each serving with a piece of fresh fruit, such as a slice of peach, or a cherry or strawberry.

Mexican Corn Pudding
(for 4)

4 ears of mature
  sweet corn
6 tbsp. sugar
½ tsp. cinnamon
½ tsp. mace

1 tsp. lemon juice
pinch of salt
3 tbsp. butter, melted
2 eggs

Score corn with a fork and scrape with a spoon to remove all the pulp from the kernels. Put the pulp in a bowl and mix with sugar, cinnamon, mace, lemon juice and salt. Beat the egg yolks and add, together with the butter, to the corn and blend. Beat the egg whites until stiff, fold into the corn mixture. Put mixture in a casserole or 1 quart soufflé dish, place dish in a larger pan half filled with water and bake at 325° for one hour or longer, until pudding is firm.

Milk Pudding
(Dulce de Leche)
(for 6)

1 cup sugar
6 egg yolks,
   beaten until creamy
3 cups milk
1 cup light cream
⅛ tsp. vanilla

$\frac{1}{3}$ cup blanched almonds,
   ground or pounded fine
¼ cup mango meat,
   diced small
¼ cup crushed, drained
   pineapple

    Combine sugar, egg yolks, milk, cream and vanilla in a saucepan; heat slowly, while stirring, until mixture starts to simmer. Add almonds and continue cooking and stirring until the mixture thickens. Add fruit, cook another 2 minutes, pour into a serving bowl and chill well.

Flaming Peaches
(for 4)

4 tbsp. butter

$^2/_3$ cup light brown sugar

1 tbsp. lemon juice

4 tbsp. tequila

4 large, firm ripe peaches, skinned and sliced

pinch of salt

4 tbsp. light rum

Heat butter in a chafing dish, add sugar, lemon juice and salt and heat, while stirring, until sugar is dissolved. Add the peaches and sauté until peaches are hot. Spoon sauce over the peaches while cooking. Pour the warmed liquors over the peaches, ignite and serve.

Pineapple Yucatan
(for 4)

8 slices fresh pineapple
(drained canned may
be used)
4 tbsp. lime juice
½ cup light brown sugar

6 tbsp. butter
¼ cup light rum
or tequila
vanilla ice cream

Sprinkle pineapple slices with lime juice. Coat with sugar and sauté in hot butter in a chafing dish or skillet, a few at a time, until browned. Return all to chafing dish, heat through, pour rum over them and ignite. Remove the slices, reduce the sauce quickly, and spoon over pineapple. Serve with ice cream.

Sherbet Acapulco
(for 4)

1½ pints lemon sherbet
¼ cup lime juice
   (or more to taste)

4 tbsp. light rum
4 tbsp. tequila
fresh grapefruit sections

Soften sherbet somewhat, add lime juice, rum and tequila, blend well and refreeze. Serve in individual cups garnished with fresh grapefruit segments.

Bloody Bull

1½ ounces tequila
2 ounces tomato juice
2 ounces canned beef bouillon
pepper and salt to taste

worcestershire sauce to taste
dash of tabasco
slice of lime

Pour tequila, tomato juice and bouillon over ice in a tall glass, add seasonings to taste. Stir well to chill and float a lime slice on top.

Sangrita
(for 4 to 6)

1 cup tomato juice
½ cup orange juice
1 ounce lime juice
1 tbsp. worcestershire sauce

¼ tsp. tabasco
1 tsp. grated onion
1 tsp. salt
8 ounces tequila

Shake all ingredients until well blended and chill. When serving put a couple of ice cubes in each glass, pour the sangrita over them.

Yucatan

1 jigger pineapple juice
½ jigger creme de menthe
   (green)
1 jigger tequila

crushed ice
1 small chunk of pineapple
1 green maraschino cherry

Put pineapple juice, creme de menthe and tequila in a shaker, add ice and shake well. Strain into a cocktail glass and garnish with pineapple and cherry.

Tequila Sour

1 ½ ounces tequila
½ ounce lemon juice
dash of bitters

1 tsp. sugar
½ slice lemon or orange
maraschino cherry

Shake tequila, lemon juice, bitters and sugar with ice. Strain into a chilled whiskey sour glass, garnish with orange or lemon slice and cherry.

Margarita

3 parts tequila
1 part cointreau
juice of ½ lime

Pour over crushed ice, stir well. Rub the rim of the glass with the rind of the lime and sprinkle the rim with salt. Strain drink into the glass.

Pineapple Punch

6 cups pineapple juice
1½ cups fresh orange juice
¼ cup lime juice
¼ cup lemon juice
½ cup sugar
1 cup dry white wine

1 cup water
2 or 3 sticks cinnamon
8 cloves
¼ tsp. mace
½ tsp. allspice

Combine sugar and water, bring to simmer, add cinnamon, cloves mace and allspice and simmer for half an hour. Strain the liquid and combine with all other ingredients. Mix well and chill.

Mexican Chocolate

(for 6)

4 cups milk
4 ounces (squares) Mexican
  chocolate, grated
½ cup cream

2 tbsp. sugar
½ tsp. powdered mace
½ (scant) tsp. cinnamon
1 egg yolk

Heat 1 cup milk, add the chocolate and stir until chocolate dissolves. Add the remainder of the milk. Blend egg yolk with cream, sugar, mace and cinnamon. Add to the hot milk and bring to the simmering point. Stir constantly while heating. When hot remove from fire, beat with a wire whisk or electric mixer until a layer of foam forms on the chocolate, then serve immediately.

Note: If Mexican chocolate is not available, use semi-sweet chocolate and sweeten to taste with sugar.

Index